Shelly the Sea Turtle
And the plastic bag
AF230930
By Christine & Edmund Leger

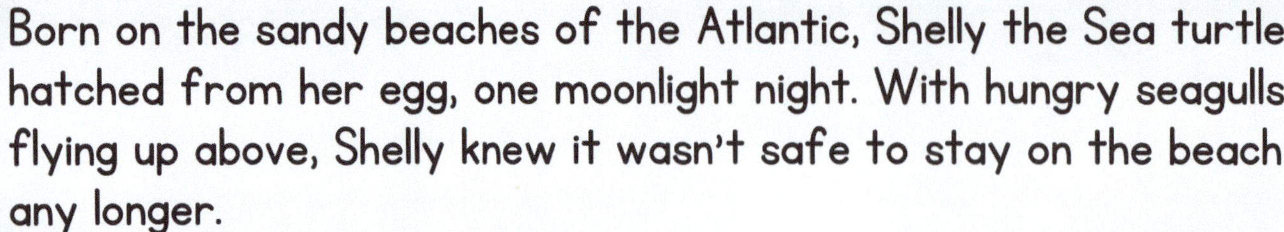
Born on the sandy beaches of the Atlantic, Shelly the Sea turtle hatched from her egg, one moonlight night. With hungry seagulls flying up above, Shelly knew it wasn't safe to stay on the beach any longer.

1

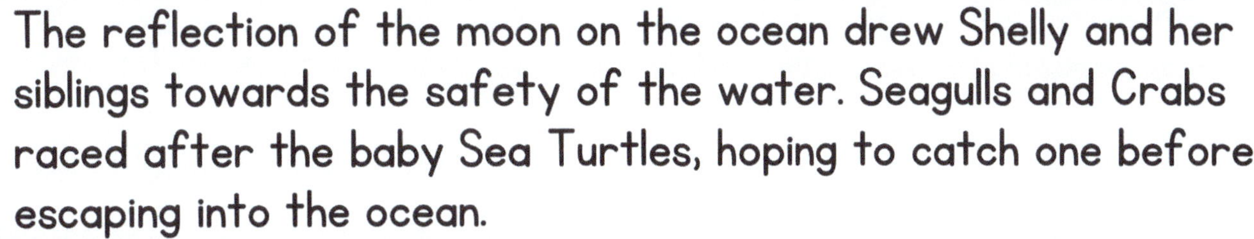

The reflection of the moon on the ocean drew Shelly and her siblings towards the safety of the water. Seagulls and Crabs raced after the baby Sea Turtles, hoping to catch one before escaping into the ocean.

Once Shelly and her siblings were safely in the water, they said their goodbyes and swam in different directions. Shelly knew that she was on her own, looking for food.

3

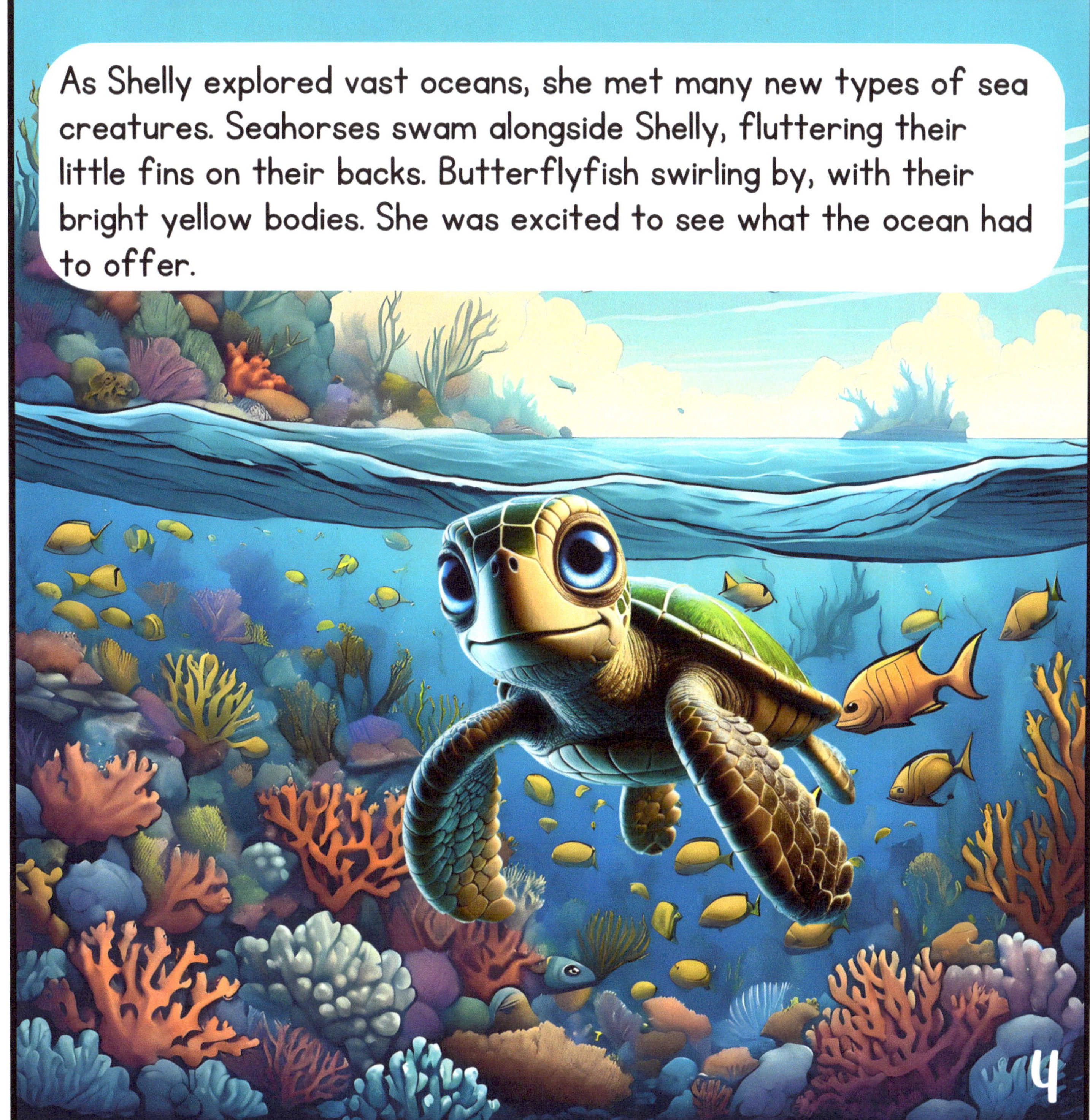

As Shelly explored vast oceans, she met many new types of sea creatures. Seahorses swam alongside Shelly, fluttering their little fins on their backs. Butterflyfish swirling by, with their bright yellow bodies. She was excited to see what the ocean had to offer.
4

For years, Shelly wandered the oceans alone. Traveling around the world, Shelly swam with Whalesharks, Jellyfish, and Sea Stars.

Just as the moonlight reflecting off the ocean surface caught Shelly's attention all those years ago, something was floating in the water that shone and caught her eyes.

As she swam closer, she could smell a tasty smell coming from the shiny object.

Shelly had never seen a sea creature like this before. She got closer to it and took a lick. It tasted a little like algae, but it was bitter. As the currents moved the object around and around in the water, Shelly became wrapped up in it.

The more she moved, the tighter it got around her shell and flippers. She started to panic. She let out a giant cry for help and tried to swim away.

Hearing her cries, a school of fish swam up to Shelly. Shelly was trying to swim to the surface, she had been underwater for far too long and needed to breathe. She pulled and pulled and tried to flap her flipper to swim, but it was no use. Her flipper was stuck to her body by this mysterious shiny thing.

The fish used their tiny teeth and chewed some of the shiny object to free Shelly's flipper.

Shelly felt her flipper become free, and swam up to the surface for a big breath of air. That is when she noticed her flipper was hurt. The shiny object was wrapped so tightly around her, that it started to cut her flipper. She was hurt and didn't know how to take the rest off of her beautiful shell.

10

For days, Shelly swam with the shiny thing wrapped around her. It was hard for her to eat because it was squeezing her tummy. As the days went by, Shelly grew more and more tired. It was becoming harder and harder for her to keep swimming, and keep her head above water to breathe.

Shelly heard rumours from other sea animals about a group of land creatures known to help injured turtles. She swam and swam, with every last bit of energy, until she found a beach –the home of the Land-creatures.

Shelly waited on a rock in the water until the sun came up. In the distance, she could hear loud noises coming from the beach. She knew no other sea animal that made that noise; it must be the land creatures. She used the last of her energy to swim herself to shore and let the waves take her in.

It was a bright and early morning for the children to be playing on the beach, but they were glad they did. As they noticed Shelly coming in from the ocean, they started to shout out for their parents to come look. At first, they didn't notice the plastic around Shelly's body.

But as they got closer, the parents soon realized why Shelly had beached herself. The plastic wrapped around her shell was getting tighter and tighter as she breathed, and the cuts on her fin that would have made swimming her hard and painful.

They worked together to load Shelly into the back of one man's truck. They padded it down with blankets and strapped her in so she wouldn't wiggle too much. And they took the slow, short trip to a very special place.

Shelly was brought to a Marine research and rehabilitation centre in the next town over. They take care of all kinds of Ocean animals that get hurt or sick in the wild.

16

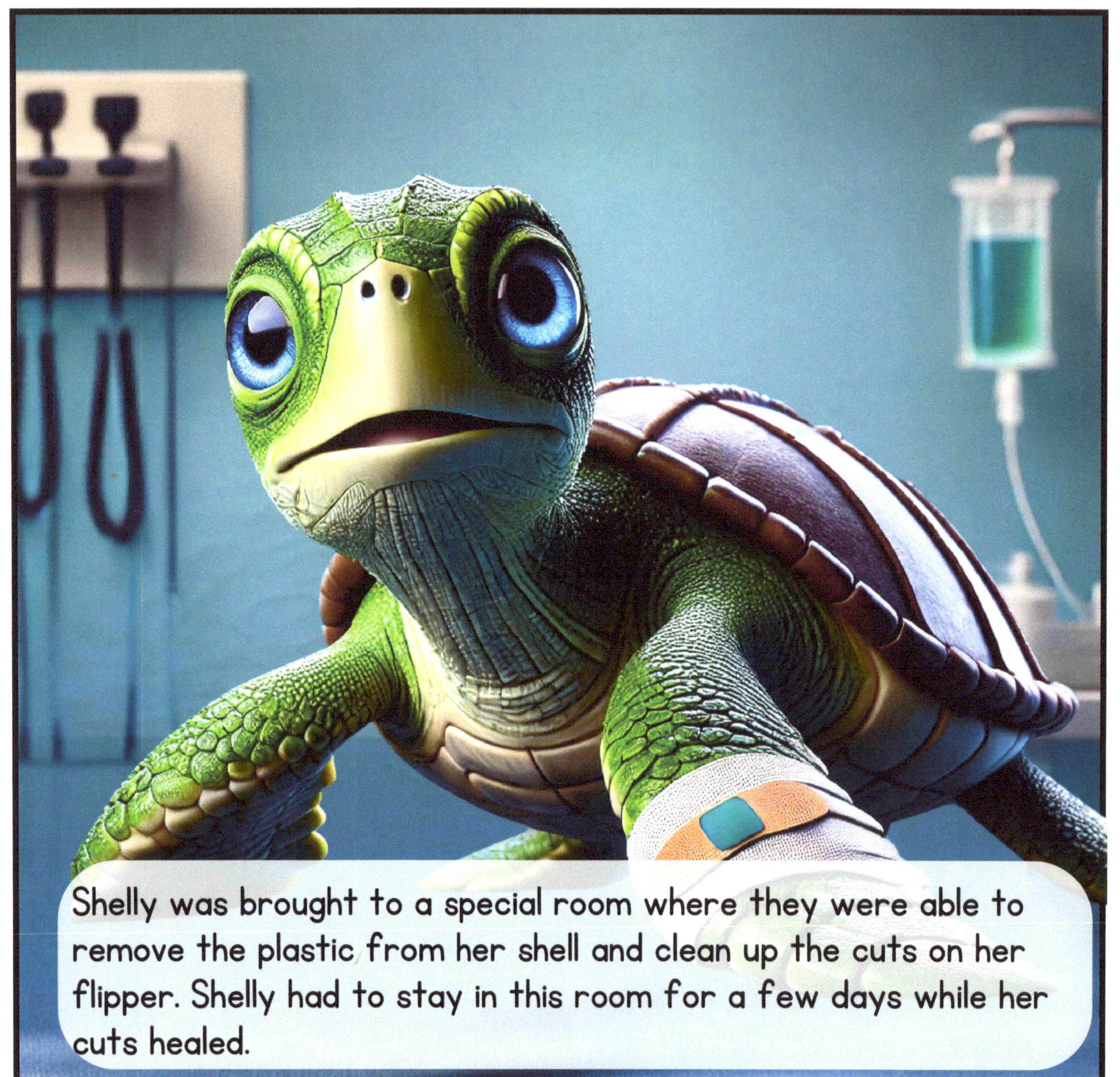

Shelly was brought to a special room where they were able to remove the plastic from her shell and clean up the cuts on her flipper. Shelly had to stay in this room for a few days while her cuts healed.

The entire town was talking about Shelly and her amazing journey to the beach. They had never seen a Turtle "asking for help" like this before.

Shelly was grateful for all the help the humans did to get her better. But she wanted to get back into the ocean. The tanks in the centre were great, but she needed more space.

There were a few other sea turtles in the centre as well. They had been injured and rescued, or kept as pets and taken away when they got too big for their enclosures. Shelly didn't want to stay at the Centre forever. She wanted to be free.

To honour Shelly and her brave journey, the local townspeople put on a Beach clean-up. They spent the day cleaning up the whole length of the beach; it passed through many towns. Soon, others started to join.

20

After months of being in the Centre, Shelly was finally able to go back to the Ocean. Since no one knew where she came from, they placed her back in the spot they found her. On their beloved, newly clean beach. "Shelly's Spot" a new sign read.

21

From there, Shelly took her time. She looked around at all the wonderful humans that had helped her. The children visited her every day and dropped snacks in her tank when the adults weren't looking.

She took one large breath, and let the waves take her away. Finally, Shelly was home.

Before they released her, the biologists from the Centre added a satellite tracker to her shell. They wanted to be able to track her around the world.
A new section of the Centres website was dedicated to tracking Shelly, and anyone could watch along if they wanted.
23

Shelly swam down the coast of South America and turned
around to swim up the western coast.

Shelly swam over 16,000 km that year. She crossed the Pacific Ocean and explored the oceans around Australia and Africa. She swam through storms and currents. She heard the loud ships and dove far underwater to stay clear of them. She loved the humans at the centre, but was in no rush to see them again.

26

Sea Turtle Facts

Sea turtles can lay up to 115 eggs, every 2-3 years.

The Green Sea Turtle is the only herbivorous (plant-eating) sea turtle species. They primarily feed on seagrasses and algae in shallow waters, which gives their fat a greenish color and their name.

5-13 million metric tons of plastic waste are dumped into the ocean, annually. When they degrade, they turn into micro-plastics. When Sea Turtles eat these micro-palstics, it can cause damage to their insides or make them feel too full to eat real food.

Sea turtles can swim up to 35km/hr when escaping a predator

Sea Turtle Facts

They grow up to 1.5 meters (5 ft) in length and can weigh over 300 kg (700 lbs), making them the largest of the hardshell sea turtles.

Just like your bones, a turtle's shell is actually part of its skeleton. It's made up of over 50 bones which include the turtle's rib cage and spine.

Sea turtles return to the beach they were hatched from, in order to lay their eggs

Sea Turtles Can Live Up To 50 Years

Sea Turtles can rest for up to five hours underwater before coming up to breathe.

www.ingramcontent.com/pod-product-compliance
Lightning Source LLC
Chambersburg PA
CBHW042137030726
47599CB00002B/512